Hani Bashier

Onboarding

Induction and Motivation

2024

Publisher:

Säästva OÜ
Hani Bashier
Tartu mnt 67/1-3B
Tallinn
Harju County
10115
https://hani.ee
hani@hani.ee

Library of Congress Control Number:
© Hani Bashier

Table of Contents

Chapter One: Onboarding, Induction and Motivation

Welcome to "On-Boarding: Induction and Motivation," where the journey of welcoming new employees into an organization is transformed into an artful process of integration and inspiration. In this book, we delve into the pivotal role of the Onboarding Professional, the orchestrator of seamless transitions and the architect of a motivated workforce. Through unique perspectives and innovative approaches, let's explore the nuances of onboarding that go beyond the conventional norms, paving the way for a new era of employee induction.

Useful Terms:

Onboarding: The process of integrating a new employee into the organization, providing them with the necessary information, tools, and support to succeed in their role.

Orientation: An initial introduction to the company and its policies, procedures, and expectations, typically conducted when a new employee joins the organization.

Training: The process of developing skills, knowledge, and competencies required to perform a job effectively through structured learning activities.

Induction: The formal process of welcoming and integrating a new employee into the organization, helping them understand the company's values, mission, and culture.

Company Culture: The shared values, beliefs, and practices that shape the behavior and interactions of employees within an organization.

Welcome Kit: A package of materials given to new employees upon joining the organization, typically containing information about the company, its policies, and some branded items.

Job Description: A document outlining the duties, responsibilities, qualifications, and expectations associated with a specific job role within the organization.

Performance Expectations: Clear and specific goals, targets, and standards that employees are expected to meet in their roles to contribute to the overall success of the organization.

Mentorship: A supportive relationship between an experienced employee (mentor) and a less experienced employee (mentee) aimed at sharing knowledge, providing guidance, and fostering professional development.

Feedback: Constructive information provided to employees about their performance, behavior, or work quality, with the aim of improving performance and achieving organizational goals.

Career Development: The process of planning and implementing strategies to help employees enhance their skills, gain new experiences, and advance their careers within the organization.

Team Building: Activities and initiatives designed to foster collaboration, communication, and trust among team members to improve teamwork and performance.

Engagement: The emotional commitment and involvement of employees towards their work, team, and organization, leading to increased productivity, satisfaction, and retention.

Benefits Package: The set of perks, incentives, and rewards offered by an organization to its employees in addition to their salary, such as health insurance, retirement plans, and paid time off.

Company Policies: Rules, guidelines, and regulations established by the organization to govern employee behavior, decision-making, and interactions within the workplace.

Goal Setting: The process of defining objectives, targets, and milestones that employees strive to achieve, aligning individual goals with the organization's strategic objectives.

Recognition: Acknowledgment and appreciation of employee contributions, achievements, and efforts to motivate and reinforce positive behavior and performance.

Growth Opportunities: Career development prospects, training programs, and advancement possibilities available to employees to enhance their skills, knowledge, and professional development.

Work-Life Balance: The equilibrium between work responsibilities and personal life, ensuring that employees have time for relaxation, hobbies, family, and other non-work activities.

Motivation: The inner drive, enthusiasm, and determination that inspires employees to work towards their goals, overcome challenges, and achieve success in their roles.

Useful Abbreviations

A&P	Advertising and Promotion
API	Application Programming Interface
ATS	Applicant Tracking System
B2B	Business to Business
B2C	Business to Consumer
BCP	Business Continuity Plan
COB	Close of Business
CPD	Continuous Professional Development
CRM	Customer Relationship Management
CTA	Call to Action
D&I	Diversity and Inclusion
EAP	Employee Assistance Program
EEO	Equal Employment Opportunity
EEOC	Equal Employment Opportunity Commission
FAQ	Frequently Asked Questions
FMLA	Family and Medical Leave Act
H&S	Health and Safety
HR	Human Resources
HRM	Human Resources Management

I9	Employment Eligibility Verification
IP	Intellectual Property
KPI	Key Performance Indicator
KRA	Key Result Area
LMS	Learning Management System
NDA	Non-Disclosure Agreement
OHS	Occupational Health and Safety
OJT	On-the-Job Training
OOO	Out of Office
OT	Overtime
P&L	Profit and Loss
PIP	Performance Improvement Plan
PIP	Personal Improvement Plan
PMP	Performance Management Process
PMP	Project Management Professional
PTO	Paid Time Off
QA	Quality Assurance
R&R	Recognition and Rewards
RFP	Request for Proposal
ROI	Return on Investment
SEO	Search Engine Optimization
SLA	Service Level Agreement
SMB	Small and Medium sized Business
SOP	Standard Operating Procedure
SOW	Statement of Work

SWOT	Strengths, Weaknesses, Opportunities, Threats
TOS	Terms of Service
UI/UX	User Interface/User Experience
VAR	Value Added Reseller
VTO	Voluntary Time Off
WFH	Work From Home

Chapter Two: The Art of Seamless Integration

Crafting a Customized Onboarding Experience

In the realm of onboarding, where the journey of welcoming new employees begins, the key to success lies in creating a customized experience that resonates with everyone. This section, titled "Crafting a Customized Onboarding Experience," delves into the art of tailoring onboarding programs to meet the unique needs and expectations of new hires, setting the stage for a seamless integration process.

As the Onboarding Professional, your role transcends the traditional boundaries of induction by embracing the diversity and individuality of each new employee. The first step in crafting a customized onboarding experience is to understand that one size does not fit all. Each recruit brings a distinct set of skills, experiences, and aspirations to the table, and it is your responsibility to ensure that their onboarding journey reflects their uniqueness.

The foundation of a customized onboarding experience begins with thorough research and preparation. Before the new hires even step through the doors of the organization, take the time to gather information about their backgrounds, interests, and career goals. This initial phase sets the tone for a personalized onboarding journey that is tailored to meet their specific needs.

Once you have gathered the necessary insights, it's time to design a roadmap for their onboarding experience. This roadmap should outline a series of activities, training sessions, and interactions that are curated to align with the individual preferences and learning styles of each new employee. By taking a personalized approach to onboarding, you not only demonstrate your commitment to their success but also lay the foundation for a lasting and meaningful connection.

In crafting a customized onboarding experience, communication is key. Keep the lines of communication open with the new hires from the very beginning, ensuring that they are aware of what to expect during the onboarding process. By setting clear expectations and being transparent about the goals and objectives of their onboarding journey, you create a sense of trust and engagement that is essential for a successful integration.

Furthermore, leverage the expertise of various departments within the organization to enhance the customized onboarding experience. Collaborate with HR colleagues, training specialists, and team leaders to tailor onboarding activities that align with the specific roles and responsibilities of the new hires. By involving key stakeholders in the onboarding process, you not only enrich the experience but also foster a sense of belonging and connection from day one.

In conclusion, crafting a customized onboarding experience is an art that requires a blend of empathy, creativity, and strategic thinking. By understanding the unique needs and aspirations of each new hire, designing personalized onboarding journeys, and fostering open communication and collaboration, you pave the way for a seamless integration process that sets the stage for long-term success and motivation. Embrace the power of customization in onboarding and watch as new employees flourish and thrive in their new roles within the organization.

Leveraging Technology for Enhanced Onboarding

In the realm of onboarding, where the convergence of technology and human connection shapes the landscape of employee integration, the utilization of cutting-edge tools and digital platforms plays a pivotal role in enhancing the onboarding experience. This section, titled "Leveraging Technology for Enhanced Onboarding," explores the innovative ways in which technology can be harnessed to elevate the onboarding process to new heights, fostering engagement, efficiency, and empowerment.

As the Onboarding Professional, you are at the forefront of embracing technological advancements to streamline onboarding procedures and create a seamless transition for new hires. The integration of technology not only modernizes the onboarding experience but also enriches it with interactive elements, personalized content, and real-time feedback mechanisms that cater to the diverse needs of today's workforce.

One of the primary benefits of leveraging technology for enhanced onboarding is the ability to deliver information and training in a dynamic and engaging manner. Traditional onboarding methods, such as lengthy orientation sessions and paper-based materials, are gradually being replaced by interactive e-learning platforms, virtual reality simulations, and mobile applications that offer a more immersive and interactive learning experience.

By incorporating multimedia elements, gamified activities, and self-paced modules into the onboarding process, new hires are empowered to navigate their training at their own pace, enhancing retention and understanding of key concepts. Through technology-enabled learning, employees can access resources anytime, anywhere, fostering a culture of continuous learning and development.

Moreover, technology serves as a bridge that connects new hires with the broader organizational ecosystem, facilitating communication, collaboration, and community-building. Virtual communication tools, such as video conferencing, instant messaging, and social intranet platforms, enable new employees to connect with their peers, mentors, and leaders, breaking down geographical barriers and fostering a sense of belonging from day one.

Another key aspect of leveraging technology for enhanced onboarding is the use of data and analytics to measure and optimize the onboarding process. By tracking key metrics, such as completion rates, engagement levels, and feedback scores, Onboarding Professionals can gain valuable insights into the effectiveness of onboarding initiatives, identify areas for improvement, and tailor future programs to better meet the needs of new hires.

In conclusion, the integration of technology into the onboarding process represents a transformative shift in how organizations welcome and integrate new employees. By leveraging digital tools, interactive platforms, and data-driven insights, Onboarding Professionals can create a personalized, engaging, and efficient onboarding experience that sets the stage for long-term success and motivation. Embrace the power of technology in onboarding, and watch as new hires embark on their journey with confidence, enthusiasm, and a sense of empowerment in their new roles.

Nurturing a Culture of Inclusivity and Belonging

In the realm of onboarding, where the foundation of a thriving organizational culture is laid, the nurturing of inclusivity and belonging emerges as a cornerstone of success. This section, titled "Nurturing a Culture of Inclusivity and Belonging," delves into the vital role that fostering a sense of community, respect, and acceptance plays in creating a supportive environment for new hires to thrive and contribute their best selves to the organization.

As the Onboarding Professional, your responsibility extends beyond the logistics of orientation and training to cultivating a culture where every individual feels valued, respected, and included. The journey of nurturing inclusivity and belonging begins from the moment a new employee walks through the doors, setting the tone for their integration and long-term engagement within the organization.

At the heart of nurturing a culture of inclusivity and belonging lies the commitment to diversity and equity. Embrace the unique backgrounds, perspectives, and experiences that each new hire brings to the table, recognizing that diversity is not only a source of strength but also a catalyst for innovation and creativity. By championing diversity and creating a safe and welcoming space for all employees, you lay the groundwork for a culture that celebrates differences and fosters a sense of belonging for everyone.

Communication plays a pivotal role in nurturing inclusivity and belonging within the organization. Encourage open dialogue, active listening, and empathy among team members to create a culture of mutual respect and understanding. Provide opportunities for new hires to share their stories, voice their opinions, and contribute their ideas, creating a sense of ownership and empowerment that fosters a strong sense of belonging.

In addition to fostering open communication, create channels for feedback and collaboration that empower employees to participate in shaping the organizational culture. Implement regular pulse surveys, focus groups, and feedback mechanisms to gather insights from new hires on their onboarding experience, work environment, and sense of inclusion. By listening to their feedback and taking action to address their concerns, you demonstrate a commitment to creating an inclusive and supportive workplace where every voice is heard and valued.

Moreover, led by example in promoting inclusivity and belonging within the organization. Ensure that policies, practices, and behaviors align with the values of diversity, equity, and inclusion, setting a standard of respect and acceptance for all employees. Encourage leaders and team members to embrace diversity, challenge biases, and champion inclusivity in their daily interactions, creating a culture where everyone feels respected, supported, and valued for who they are.

In conclusion, nurturing a culture of inclusivity and belonging is not just a goal to strive for but a commitment to uphold in every aspect of the onboarding journey. By championing diversity, fostering open communication, empowering employees to share their voices, and leading by example in promoting inclusivity, Onboarding Professionals can create a culture where every individual feels welcomed, respected, and valued. Embrace the power of inclusivity and belonging in onboarding, and watch as new hires flourish, thrive, and contribute their unique talents to the collective success of the organization.

Chapter Three: Steps to Implement Onboarding Terms

Onboarding

1) Develop a comprehensive onboarding plan that outlines the training, orientation, and support new employees will receive.
2) Provide new hires with all necessary information, resources, and tools to succeed in their roles.
3) Assign a buddy or mentor to guide and support the new employee during the onboarding process.

4) Set clear expectations and goals for the onboarding period to help new employees acclimate to the organization.

Orientation

1) Schedule a formal orientation session to introduce new employees to the company's history, mission, values, and culture.
2) Provide an overview of company policies, procedures, benefits, and expectations during the orientation session.
3) Introduce new hires to key team members and stakeholders to facilitate networking and relationship-building.
4) Offer a tour of the workplace and facilities to familiarize new employees with their surroundings.

Training

1) Identify the specific skills, knowledge, and competencies required for each job role within the organization.
2) Develop a training program that incorporates a mix of on-the-job training, classroom instruction, and e-learning modules.
3) Assign trainers or subject matter experts to deliver training sessions and provide hands-on guidance to employees.
4) Evaluate training effectiveness through assessments, quizzes, and feedback to ensure employees have mastered the required skills.

1) Create a structured induction program that introduces new employees to the organization's mission, vision, values, and culture.
2) Assign a mentor or buddy to support new employees during the induction period and help them navigate the organization.
3) Provide opportunities for new hires to meet with key stakeholders, department heads, and team members to build connections.
4) Gather feedback from new employees about their induction experience to continuously improve the process.

Company Culture

1) Define and communicate the organization's core values, beliefs, and behaviors that shape its unique culture.
2) Lead by example and encourage leadership and employees to embody the company culture in their daily actions and decisions.
3) Promote open communication, collaboration, and inclusivity to foster a positive and engaging work environment.
4) Recognize and reward employees who exemplify the company culture and contribute to a positive workplace atmosphere.

Welcome Kit

1) Gather necessary materials, such as company information, policies, and branded items.

2) Personalize the welcome kit with a welcome note or message from the team.
3) Present the welcome kit to new employees on their first day or during orientation.
4) Follow up with new hires to ensure they have everything they need and address any questions or concerns.

Job Description

1) Define the role's responsibilities, duties, and objectives.
2) Specify the qualifications, skills, and experience required for the position.
3) Review and update the job description regularly to align with changing organizational needs.
4) Share the job description with candidates during recruitment and with employees to clarify expectations.

Performance Expectations

1) Set clear, specific, and measurable performance goals for each employee.
2) Communicate performance expectations effectively, ensuring understanding and alignment.
3) Provide regular feedback and coaching to help employees meet and exceed performance expectations.
4) Conduct performance evaluations to assess progress and adjust expectations as needed.

Mentorship

1) Identify experienced and knowledgeable employees to serve as mentors.

2) Pair mentors with mentees based on skills, goals, and areas for development.

3) Establish regular meetings and check-ins to facilitate learning, guidance, and feedback.

4) Encourage open communication and a supportive environment for mentorship to thrive.

Feedback

1) Provide timely, specific, and constructive feedback to employees on their performance.

2) Use a mix of positive reinforcement and areas for improvement in feedback.

3) Encourage a feedback culture where employees feel comfortable giving and receiving feedback.

4) Follow up on feedback with action plans and support to help employees grow and develop.

Career Development

1) Identify employees' career goals, aspirations, and development needs.

2) Create individual development plans that outline goals, actions, and timelines for career growth.

3) Offer training, mentoring, job rotations, and stretch assignments to support career development.

4) Regularly review and adjust career development plans to ensure alignment with employee aspirations and organizational objectives.

Team Building

1) Identify team strengths, weaknesses, and dynamics.

2) Plan team-building activities to foster trust, communication, and collaboration.
3) Encourage participation and engagement in team-building exercises.
4) Reflect on the outcomes and learnings from team-building activities to strengthen team bonds.

Engagement

1) Communicate openly and transparently with employees about the organization's goals and vision.
2) Provide opportunities for employees to contribute ideas, feedback, and suggestions.
3) Recognize and appreciate employee contributions and achievements.
4) Foster a positive work environment that values employee well-being and professional growth.

Benefits Package

1) Determine the needs and preferences of employees regarding benefits.
2) Research and select a comprehensive benefits package that aligns with employee needs and company resources.
3) Communicate the benefits package clearly to employees and provide support for enrollment and utilization.
4) Regularly review and update the benefits package to ensure it remains competitive and meets employee expectations.

1) Develop a clear and comprehensive set of company policies that align with legal requirements and organizational values.
2) Communicate company policies to employees through handbooks, training sessions, and regular updates.
3) Provide guidance and support to employees in understanding and adhering to company policies.
4) Monitor compliance with company policies and address any issues or concerns promptly and fairly.

1) Define specific, measurable, achievable, relevant, and time-bound (SMART) goals for individuals and teams.
2) Align goals with the organization's strategic objectives and priorities.
3) Collaborate with employees to set goals that motivate and challenge them to excel.
4) Monitor progress, provide feedback, and adjust goals as needed to drive performance and success.

1) Establish a formal recognition program that celebrates employee achievements and contributions.
2) Encourage peer-to-peer recognition to foster a culture of appreciation and support.
3) Personalize recognition efforts to acknowledge individual strengths and accomplishments.

4) Sustain a culture of recognition by consistently acknowledging and rewarding employee efforts and successes.

Growth Opportunities

1) Conduct regular career development discussions with employees to understand their aspirations and growth areas.
2) Identify potential growth opportunities within the organization, such as training programs, job rotations, or stretch assignments.
3) Create individualized development plans that align with employees' career goals and organizational needs.
4) Provide ongoing support, feedback, and resources to help employees capitalize on growth opportunities and advance in their careers.

Work-Life Balance

1) Encourage open communication with employees to understand their work-life balance needs and preferences.
2) Promote flexible work arrangements, such as telecommuting, flexible hours, or compressed workweeks.
3) Set boundaries and encourage time management practices to help employees maintain a healthy balance between work and personal life.
4) Lead by example and cultivate a culture that values and supports work-life balance for all employees.

1) Understand the individual motivators of each employee through regular communication and feedback.
2) Set challenging yet achievable goals that align with employees' interests, skills, and aspirations.
3) Provide opportunities for growth, recognition, and learning to keep employees engaged and motivated.
4) Foster a positive work environment that values employee contributions, encourages creativity, and promotes a sense of purpose and fulfillment.

Chapter Four: Communication and Connection

The Power of Effective Verbal and Written Communication

In the realm of onboarding, where human connection serves as the bridge between new hires and organizational success, the power of effective verbal and written communication emerges as a critical element in shaping the onboarding experience. This section, titled "The Power of Effective Verbal and Written Communication," delves into the significance of clear, concise, and impactful communication in fostering understanding, engagement, and connection during the onboarding process.

As the Onboarding Professional, you wield the power of words to guide, inspire, and inform new hires as they embark on their journey within the organization. Effective communication is not merely a skill but a strategic tool that can shape perceptions, build relationships, and set the stage for success from the very beginning.

Verbal communication forms the foundation of interactions during the onboarding process, encompassing everything from welcoming new hires with warmth and enthusiasm to delivering informative presentations and conducting engaging training sessions. The art of verbal communication lies in not just conveying information but in creating a welcoming and inclusive environment where new employees feel valued, heard, and supported.

When communicating verbally with new hires, strive to be clear, concise, and approachable in your delivery. Break down complex concepts into digestible chunks, use relatable examples and stories to illustrate key points, and encourage questions and feedback to ensure understanding. By fostering open dialogue and active listening, you create a space where new hires feel comfortable asking for clarification, seeking guidance, and sharing their thoughts and ideas.

Written communication, on the other hand, plays a crucial role in providing structure, consistency, and reference points throughout the onboarding journey. From detailed welcome emails and onboarding manuals to instructional guides and feedback forms, written communication serves as a roadmap that guides new hires through the intricacies of their roles, responsibilities, and the organizational culture.

In crafting written communication for onboarding, prioritize clarity, coherence, and accessibility. Use simple language, visual aids, and bullet points to convey information efficiently and effectively. Ensure that written materials are well-organized, visually appealing, and easily navigable, enhancing the readability and retention of key information for new hires.

Moreover, harness the power of storytelling in your written communication to create a narrative that resonates with new hires on a personal level. Share success stories, testimonials from current employees, and the organization's mission, vision, and values in a compelling and engaging manner that inspires and motivates new hires to become part of something greater than themselves.

In conclusion, the power of effective verbal and written communication is not just about transmitting information but about building connections, fostering engagement, and cultivating a sense of belonging for new hires. By mastering the art of clear, concise, and impactful communication, Onboarding Professionals can create a welcoming, informative, and inspiring onboarding experience that sets the stage for long-term success and engagement. Embrace the power of communication in onboarding, and watch as new hires embark on their journey with confidence, clarity, and a deep sense of connection to the organization and its mission.

In the enchanting realm of onboarding, where the seeds of lasting connections are sown, the art of building strong relationships takes center stage. This section, titled "Building Strong Relationships Through Onboarding," delves into the profound impact that cultivating genuine connections, trust, and rapport can have on the integration and engagement of new hires within the organization.

As the Onboarding Professional, you possess the unique opportunity to foster meaningful relationships that transcend mere professional interactions and evolve into lasting partnerships built on trust, respect, and mutual understanding. The journey of building strong relationships through onboarding is not just a process but a profound art that requires empathy, authenticity, and intentionality to flourish.

At the heart of building strong relationships lies the foundation of trust. Establishing trust with new hires begins from the moment they step through the doors of the organization, greeted with warmth, sincerity, and a genuine interest in their well-being and success. Demonstrate transparency, integrity, and reliability in your interactions to instill confidence and trust in new hires, paving the way for authentic connections to blossom.

One of the key pillars of building strong relationships through onboarding is active listening. Take the time to truly listen to new hires, understand their aspirations, concerns, and expectations, and validate their experiences and perspectives. By showing empathy, compassion, and a willingness to engage in meaningful conversations, you create a safe and supportive space where new hires feel heard, valued, and respected.

In addition to active listening, personalized engagement plays a crucial role in building strong relationships during the onboarding process. Tailor the onboarding experience to meet the unique needs, preferences, and learning styles of each new hire, demonstrating a commitment to their individual growth and development within the organization. By acknowledging and celebrating the diversity of experiences and backgrounds that new hires bring to the table, you foster a sense of belonging and connection that transcends differences and unites individuals in a shared sense of purpose.

Furthermore, encourage collaboration and teamwork as a means of strengthening relationships among new hires and existing employees. Create opportunities for team-building activities, group projects, and cross-functional initiatives that enable individuals to connect, collaborate, and build camaraderie based on shared goals and values. By fostering a spirit of unity and collaboration, you not only build strong relationships within teams but also create a sense of community and belonging that transcends individual roles and responsibilities.

In conclusion, the art of building strong relationships through onboarding is a transformative journey that goes beyond mere introductions and formalities to create enduring connections that shape the fabric of the organizational culture. By fostering trust, practicing active listening, personalizing engagement, and promoting collaboration, Onboarding Professionals can cultivate a sense of community, camaraderie, and mutual support that empowers new hires to thrive, grow, and contribute their best selves to the collective success of the organization. Embrace the power of building strong relationships in onboarding and watch as new hires become not just colleagues but cherished members of a vibrant and inclusive community united by shared values, goals, and a deep sense of connection.

Harnessing the Strength of Interpersonal Skills

In the realm of onboarding, where human connections are the threads that weave the fabric of organizational success, the ability to harness the strength of interpersonal skills emerges as a potent force in shaping meaningful interactions, fostering collaboration, and nurturing a culture of engagement and excellence. This section, titled "Harnessing the Strength of Interpersonal Skills," delves into the art of cultivating empathy, communication, and emotional intelligence to create impactful and transformative onboarding experiences for new hires.

As the Onboarding Professional, you possess a unique set of interpersonal skills that serve as the cornerstone of your ability to connect, inspire, and empower new hires on their journey of integration and growth within the organization. The art of harnessing interpersonal skills is not just about communication but about building bridges of understanding, trust, and empathy that transcend individual differences and unite individuals in a shared vision of collective success.

One of the key pillars of interpersonal skills is empathy, the ability to understand and resonate with the thoughts, feelings, and experiences of others. By cultivating empathy in your interactions with new hires, you demonstrate a genuine interest in their well-being, perspectives, and aspirations, creating a foundation of trust and mutual respect that forms the bedrock of strong relationships and effective collaboration.

Effective communication is another essential component of interpersonal skills that plays a pivotal role in onboarding success. Clear, open, and transparent communication fosters clarity, alignment, and engagement among new hires, setting the stage for productive interactions, meaningful exchanges, and shared understanding. By honing your communication skills, you create a space where ideas are shared, questions are welcomed, and feedback is valued, enhancing the overall onboarding experience for new hires.

Moreover, emotional intelligence, the ability to recognize, understand, and manage emotions in oneself and others, is a critical aspect of interpersonal skills that empowers Onboarding Professionals to navigate complex interpersonal dynamics with grace and wisdom. By cultivating emotional intelligence, you develop a heightened awareness of the emotions, motivations, and needs of new hires, enabling you to tailor your interactions, support, and guidance to meet them where they are and empower them to grow and succeed.

In addition to empathy, communication, and emotional intelligence, active listening serves as a fundamental element of interpersonal skills that enhances your ability to connect with new hires on a deeper level. By listening attentively, empathetically, and non-judgmentally to the perspectives, concerns, and feedback of new hires, you demonstrate respect, validation, and a willingness to engage in meaningful dialogue that fosters trust, understanding, and collaboration.

In conclusion, the art of harnessing the strength of interpersonal skills in onboarding is a transformative journey that empowers Onboarding Professionals to create inclusive, engaging, and impactful experiences that resonate with new hires on a personal and emotional level. By cultivating empathy, honing communication, nurturing emotional intelligence, and practicing active listening, you create a space where new hires feel seen, heard, and valued, laying the foundation for meaningful connections, collaborative relationships, and a culture of excellence and growth within the organization. Embrace the power of interpersonal skills in onboarding, and watch as new hires thrive, succeed, and become integral members of a vibrant and supportive community united by shared values, goals, and a deep sense of connection and belonging.

Chapter Five: Experienced Quotes

- "The only way to do great work is to love what you do.", Steve Jobs, 2005.
- "To win in the marketplace, you must first win in the workplace.", Doug Conant, 2009.
- "Employees who believe that management is concerned about them as a whole person—not just an employee—are more productive, more satisfied, more fulfilled.", Anne M. Mulcahy, 2008
- "Culture eats strategy for breakfast.", Peter Drucker
- "The greatest asset of a company is its people.", Jorge Paulo Lemann
- "Motivation is the art of getting people to do what you want them to do because they want to do it.", Dwight D. Eisenhower, 1950s
- "You don't build a business—you build people—and then people build the business.", Zig Ziglar
- "On-boarding isn't about checking boxes. It's about welcoming, integrating, and engaging.", Susan Heathfield, 2017
- "New hires are like seedlings; they need care and attention to grow.", Alison Green, 2010s
- "A leader's job is not to do the work for others; it's to help others figure out how to do it themselves, get things done, and succeed beyond what they thought possible.", Simon Sinek, 2014
- "Employee engagement is the emotional commitment the employee has to the organization and its goals.", Kevin Kruse, 2012

- "The key to success is to start before you are ready.", Marie Forleo, 2011

- "Induction is the first impression that a new employee has of your company. It's a make-or-break moment.", Speaker: Ben Eubanks, 2018

- "A good induction program is not just a box-ticking exercise; it's a critical component of employee success.", Alan Price, 2015

- "If you want something new, you have to stop doing something old.", Peter F. Drucker, 1999

- "Motivation is what gets you started. Habit is what keeps you going.", Jim Rohn.

- "Employee orientation is a process—a means to provide the new employee with the information they need to function comfortably and effectively in the organization.", Michael Armstrong, 2010

- "A person who feels appreciated will always do more than expected."

- "The strength of the team is each individual member. The strength of each member is the team.", Phil Jackson, 1990s

- "The only way to achieve the impossible is to believe it is possible, Charles Kingsleigh (Character from "Alice in Wonderland"), 2010

Chapter Six: Continuous Improvement and Innovation

Leveraging Data and Analytics for Onboarding Success

In the ever-evolving landscape of onboarding practices, the strategic utilization of data and analytics emerges as a powerful tool for unlocking insights, optimizing processes, and driving success in the integration of new hires within the organization. This section, titled "Leveraging Data and Analytics for Onboarding Success," delves into the transformative impact of data-driven decision-making, predictive analytics, and continuous improvement on enhancing the onboarding experience and maximizing the potential of new hires.

As the Onboarding Professional, you possess a wealth of valuable data and analytics that hold the key to unlocking hidden patterns, trends, and opportunities within the onboarding process. By harnessing the power of data-driven insights, you can gain a deeper understanding of the effectiveness of current onboarding strategies, identify areas for improvement, and tailor onboarding experiences to meet the evolving needs and expectations of new hires.

One of the primary benefits of leveraging data and analytics for onboarding success is the ability to track and measure key performance indicators that provide valuable insights into the efficiency, engagement, and impact of the onboarding process. By collecting and analyzing data on metrics such as time to productivity, retention rates, and employee satisfaction, you can identify bottlenecks, gaps, and areas of strength within the onboarding journey, allowing you to make informed decisions and course corrections to enhance the overall experience for new hires.

Moreover, predictive analytics plays a crucial role in forecasting future outcomes, trends, and challenges within the onboarding process, enabling you to proactively address potential issues, optimize resource allocation, and mitigate risks before they escalate. By leveraging predictive models, machine learning algorithms, and data visualization tools, you can anticipate the needs, preferences, and performance of new hires, enabling you to tailor onboarding experiences that are personalized, impactful, and aligned with individual goals and aspirations.

In addition to tracking performance metrics and leveraging predictive analytics, continuous improvement stands at the core of leveraging data and analytics for onboarding success. By adopting a mindset of iterative learning, experimentation, and adaptation, you can embrace a culture of continuous improvement that drives innovation, agility, and excellence in the onboarding process. Use data-driven insights to inform strategic decisions, test new initiatives, and measure the impact of changes, fostering a culture of innovation and growth that propels the onboarding experience to new heights of success.

Furthermore, the integration of data and analytics with talent management strategies provides a holistic approach to onboarding that aligns individual development with organizational goals and objectives. By connecting onboarding data with talent acquisition, performance management, and learning and development initiatives, you can create a seamless and interconnected ecosystem that supports the growth, engagement, and retention of talent within the organization. By leveraging data and analytics to inform talent management decisions, you can cultivate a culture of continuous learning, development, and advancement that empowers new hires to thrive, succeed, and contribute their best selves to the collective success of the organization.

In conclusion, the art of leveraging data and analytics for onboarding success is a transformative journey that empowers Onboarding Professionals to make informed decisions, drive innovation, and create personalized and impactful experiences that resonate with new hires on both a strategic and individual level. By harnessing the power of data-driven insights, predictive analytics, continuous improvement, and talent management integration, you can unlock the full potential of the onboarding process, optimize performance, and nurture a culture of excellence, growth, and success within the organization. Embrace the power of data and analytics in onboarding and watch as new hires embark on a journey of discovery, growth, and achievement that propels them towards their fullest potential and aligns them with the shared vision and values of the organization.

Innovations in Onboarding Practice

"Innovations in Onboarding Practices" herald a new era of creativity, adaptability, and transformation in the realm of integrating new hires into the organizational tapestry. As the Onboarding Professional, you are at the forefront of pioneering cutting-edge approaches, technologies, and methodologies that redefine the onboarding experience, elevate engagement, and foster a culture of continuous learning and improvement.

Innovations in onboarding practices encompass a spectrum of groundbreaking initiatives that challenge traditional norms, embrace digital advancements, and prioritize the human-centric aspect of the onboarding journey. This section explores the dynamic landscape of innovative onboarding practices, from immersive onboarding experiences to gamification, virtual reality, and beyond, that revolutionize the way new hires are welcomed, supported, and empowered to succeed.

One of the key innovations in onboarding practices is the shift towards personalized and customized onboarding experiences that cater to the unique needs, preferences, and learning styles of individual new hires. By leveraging technology such as artificial intelligence, machine learning, and predictive analytics, Onboarding Professionals can create tailored onboarding journeys that align with the skill sets, aspirations, and goals of new hires, enhancing engagement, retention, and performance from the outset.

Moreover, gamification emerges as a powerful tool in engaging new hires, fostering collaboration, and enhancing knowledge retention through interactive and immersive experiences that transform the traditional onboarding process into a dynamic and engaging adventure. By incorporating gamified elements such as quizzes, challenges, and rewards into the onboarding curriculum, Onboarding Professionals can create a fun, interactive, and memorable onboarding experience that motivates new hires to learn, connect, and grow in a playful and engaging manner.

Virtual reality (VR) and augmented reality (AR) technologies represent another frontier of innovation in onboarding practices, offering new hires the opportunity to explore virtual environments, interact with digital simulations, and engage in realistic scenarios that simulate real-world challenges and opportunities. By immersing new hires in virtual onboarding experiences that replicate the workplace environment, culture, and dynamics, Onboarding Professionals can accelerate the acclimatization process, build confidence, and empower new hires to navigate their roles with ease and proficiency.

Furthermore, the integration of social learning platforms, peer-to-peer mentoring networks, and online communities into the onboarding process fosters collaboration, knowledge sharing, and relationship building among new hires, creating a sense of belonging, camaraderie, and support that transcends geographical boundaries and organizational hierarchies. By providing new hires with access to a diverse and inclusive community of peers, mentors, and resources, Onboarding Professionals can cultivate a culture of continuous learning, growth, and innovation that empowers new hires to thrive, succeed, and contribute their unique talents and perspectives to the collective success of the organization.

In conclusion, innovations in onboarding practices herald a transformative shift in the way new hires are welcomed, onboarded, and integrated into the organizational fabric. By embracing personalized onboarding experiences, gamification, virtual reality, social learning platforms, and other cutting-edge initiatives, Onboarding Professionals can create dynamic, engaging, and impactful onboarding experiences that resonate with new hires on a personal and emotional level, fostering a sense of connection, purpose, and empowerment from day one. Embrace the spirit of innovation in onboarding practices, and watch as new hires embark on a journey of discovery, growth, and achievement that propels them towards their fullest potential and aligns them with the shared vision and values of the organization.

Integrating Onboarding with Talent Management Strategies

"In Integrating Onboarding with Talent Management Strategies," we delve into the symbiotic relationship between the onboarding process and broader talent management initiatives, illuminating how the seamless integration of these two critical functions can amplify organizational success, foster employee development, and drive strategic growth. As the Onboarding Professional, you are uniquely positioned to orchestrate this harmonious fusion, aligning onboarding practices with talent management strategies to cultivate a culture of excellence, engagement, and retention within the organization.

At the heart of integrating onboarding with talent management strategies lies the recognition that successful onboarding is not merely a standalone event but a pivotal component of a larger talent management framework that spans the entire employee lifecycle. By aligning onboarding practices with talent acquisition, performance management, career development, and succession planning strategies, Onboarding Professionals can create a cohesive and interconnected ecosystem that nurtures talent, fosters growth, and cultivates a pipeline of skilled and engaged employees who are poised to drive organizational success.

One of the key benefits of integrating onboarding with talent management strategies is the seamless transition of new hires from the onboarding phase to ongoing development and career advancement opportunities within the organization. By creating a clear pathway for new hires to progress, grow, and thrive within the organizational hierarchy, Onboarding Professionals can enhance retention, engagement, and satisfaction levels among employees, fostering a sense of purpose, belonging, and long-term commitment to the organization.

Moreover, the integration of onboarding with talent management strategies enables Onboarding Professionals to leverage onboarding data, feedback, and performance metrics to inform talent development initiatives, succession planning, and leadership development programs. By capturing insights from the onboarding process and aligning them with talent management objectives, Onboarding Professionals can identify high-potential employees, nurture key talent, and create personalized development plans that align individual aspirations with organizational goals, fostering a culture of continuous learning, growth, and advancement.

Furthermore, the seamless integration of onboarding with talent management strategies facilitates the identification and mitigation of talent gaps, skill shortages, and succession risks within the organization, enabling Onboarding Professionals to proactively address talent needs, optimize resource allocation, and cultivate a diverse and skilled workforce that is agile, resilient, and future-ready. By aligning onboarding practices with talent management strategies, Onboarding Professionals can create a talent pipeline that is robust, adaptable, and responsive to changing business needs and market dynamics, ensuring that the organization remains competitive, innovative, and sustainable in the long term.

In conclusion, integrating onboarding with talent management strategies represents a strategic imperative for Onboarding Professionals seeking to optimize the onboarding experience, drive employee engagement, and align individual development with organizational objectives. By fostering a culture of integration, collaboration, and alignment between onboarding and talent management functions, Onboarding Professionals can unlock synergies, efficiencies, and opportunities that propel the organization towards excellence, growth, and success. Embrace the power of integrating onboarding with talent management strategies, and witness as new hires evolve into engaged, skilled, and motivated employees who are ready to contribute their best selves to the collective success of the organization.

Chapter Seven: Mastery and Growth

Developing HR Expertise in Onboarding Processes

In today's competitive business landscape, the importance of effective onboarding processes cannot be overstated. As organizations strive to attract and retain top talent, Human Resources (HR) professionals must develop expertise in creating and implementing seamless onboarding experiences. This section delves into the critical aspects of developing HR expertise in onboarding processes, exploring the key components, best practices, and strategies that contribute to successful employee integration.

The Significance of HR Expertise in Onboarding

Onboarding is more than just a series of administrative tasks; it's a crucial period that sets the tone for an employee's entire journey within an organization. HR professionals with expertise in onboarding processes play a pivotal role in ensuring that new hires feel welcomed, informed, and prepared to contribute effectively from day one. By mastering the art of onboarding, HR teams can significantly impact employee engagement, productivity, and long-term retention.

Strategic Planning and Design

Developing HR expertise in onboarding begins with a strategic approach to planning and designing the process. This involves:

- Aligning onboarding objectives with organizational goals
- Creating a comprehensive onboarding timeline
- Identifying key stakeholders and their roles in the process
- Developing a structured curriculum that covers all essential aspects of the job and company culture

Personalization and Customization

One size does not fit all when it comes to onboarding. HR experts understand the importance of tailoring the experience to individual needs:

- Conducting pre-onboarding assessments to understand new hire preferences and learning styles
- Customizing onboarding materials and activities based on job roles and departments
- Incorporating personalized welcome messages and introductions from team members and leadership

Technology Integration

In the digital age, HR expertise in onboarding must include proficiency in leveraging technology:

- Implementing user-friendly onboarding platforms and software
- Utilizing virtual reality (VR) or augmented reality (AR) for immersive onboarding experiences
- Incorporating gamification elements to enhance engagement and knowledge retention

Cultural Assimilation

HR experts recognize the critical role of cultural integration in successful onboarding:

- Developing programs that effectively communicate company values, mission, and vision
- Creating opportunities for new hires to connect with colleagues and build relationships
- Implementing mentorship or buddy systems to provide ongoing support and guidance

Best Practices for Developing HR Expertise in Onboarding

Continuous Learning and Development

To stay at the forefront of onboarding best practices, HR professionals should:

- Attend industry conferences and workshops focused on onboarding trends
- Participate in online courses and webinars to enhance skills and knowledge
- Stay updated on the latest research and literature in the field of employee onboarding

Data-Driven Decision Making

HR experts leverage data to refine and improve onboarding processes:

- Implementing metrics and KPIs to measure onboarding effectiveness
- Conducting regular surveys and feedback sessions with new hires and managers
- Analyzing data to identify areas for improvement and make informed decisions

Cross-Functional Collaboration

Effective onboarding requires collaboration across various departments:

- Building strong partnerships with IT, facilities, and other relevant teams
- Involving department heads and team leaders in the onboarding process design
- Facilitating open communication channels between HR and other business units

Embracing Innovation and Flexibility

HR experts in onboarding are open to new ideas and approaches:

- Experimenting with innovative onboarding techniques and methodologies
- Adapting processes to accommodate remote and hybrid work environments
- Staying agile and responsive to changing organizational needs and employee expectations

Develop a Comprehensive Onboarding Toolkit

- Create a robust set of resources and tools to support the onboarding process:
- Design templates for onboarding checklists, schedules, and welcome packets
- Develop interactive training modules and e-learning courses
- Create a repository of best practices and case studies for reference

Establish an Onboarding Center of Excellence

Foster a culture of expertise within the HR team:

- Designate onboarding specialists or champions within the HR department
- Create a knowledge-sharing platform for HR professionals to exchange ideas and experiences
- Implement a mentorship program for junior HR staff to learn from seasoned onboarding experts

Collaborate with Industry Partners and Experts

Expand knowledge and perspectives through external collaborations:

- Partner with universities or research institutions to stay informed about the latest onboarding trends
- Engage with onboarding consultants or experts for specialized insights and guidance

- Participate in industry working groups or committees focused on onboarding best practices

Implement Continuous Improvement Processes

Foster a culture of ongoing refinement and enhancement:

- Conduct regular audits of the onboarding process to identify areas for improvement
- Implement a feedback loop that incorporates insights from new hires, managers, and HR team members
- Regularly update and refresh onboarding materials and programs to reflect evolving best practices

Developing HR expertise in onboarding processes is a critical investment for organizations seeking to create positive first impressions and set new employees up for long-term success. By focusing on strategic planning, personalization, technology integration, and cultural assimilation, HR professionals can create onboarding experiences that not only welcome new hires but also inspire them to become fully engaged and productive members of the organization. Through continuous learning, data-driven decision-making, cross-functional collaboration, and a commitment to innovation, HR teams can elevate their onboarding expertise and contribute significantly to organizational success in the competitive landscape of talent acquisition and retention.

In today's rapidly evolving business landscape, the ability to embrace change and foster resilience is crucial for successful onboarding processes. As organizations face unprecedented challenges and opportunities, HR professionals must adapt their onboarding strategies to ensure new hires are equipped to thrive in dynamic environments. This section explores the importance of change management and resilience in onboarding, providing insights and strategies for creating adaptable and robust onboarding experiences.

The Need for Change and Resilience in Onboarding

Adapting to a Dynamic Business Environment

The business world is constantly evolving, driven by technological advancements, shifting market demands, and global events. Onboarding processes must reflect this reality, preparing new hires for a workplace characterized by change and uncertainty. By incorporating change management principles into onboarding, organizations can help employees develop the mindset and skills necessary to navigate evolving business landscapes.

Building Resilient Workforces

Resilience is the ability to bounce back from setbacks, adapt to change, and thrive in the face of adversity. In today's challenging business environment, resilient employees are more valuable than ever. Onboarding presents a unique opportunity to instill resilience in new hires from the outset, setting them up for long-term success within the organization.

Strategies for Embracing Change in Onboarding

Flexible Onboarding Structures

Develop onboarding programs that can easily adapt to changing circumstances:

- Create modular onboarding content that can be rearranged or updated as needed
- Implement agile methodologies in onboarding design and delivery
- Establish feedback loops to quickly identify and address emerging needs

Emphasize Adaptability in Company Culture

Integrate the importance of adaptability into the onboarding curriculum:

- Highlight company values that promote innovation and flexibility
- Share stories of how the organization has successfully navigated past changes
- Encourage new hires to contribute fresh perspectives and ideas

Incorporate Change Management Principles

Introduce change management concepts during the onboarding process:

- Educate new hires on common change models and frameworks

- Provide tools and techniques for managing personal and organizational change
- Discuss the role of change agents within the company

Leverage Technology for Dynamic Onboarding

Utilize technology to create adaptable onboarding experiences:

- Implement learning management systems that allow for easy content updates
- Use virtual and augmented reality to simulate various workplace scenarios
- Incorporate AI-driven personalization to tailor onboarding to individual needs

Fostering Resilience Through Onboarding

Develop a Growth Mindset

Encourage new hires to embrace challenges and view setbacks as opportunities for growth:

- Introduce the concept of a growth mindset during onboarding sessions
- Share examples of how failures have led to innovations within the company
- Provide resources for continuous learning and skill development

Build Strong Support Networks

Help new employees establish connections that can provide support during challenging times:

- Implement mentorship programs as part of the onboarding process
- Facilitate peer-to-peer networking opportunities
- Introduce new hires to key stakeholders and support personnel across the organization

Teach Stress Management and Well-being Techniques

Equip new employees with tools to manage stress and maintain well-being:

- Incorporate mindfulness and stress reduction techniques into onboarding activities
- Provide information on company wellness programs and resources
- Encourage work-life balance from the start of employment

Simulate Challenging Scenarios

Prepare new hires for potential obstacles through simulated experiences:

- Use role-playing exercises to practice problem-solving in difficult situations
- Incorporate case studies of past challenges and how they were overcome
- Utilize gamification to create engaging, scenario-based learning experiences

Measuring the Impact of Change and Resilience in Onboarding

Establish Key Performance Indicators (KPIs)

Develop metrics to assess the effectiveness of change and resilience initiatives in onboarding:

- Employee adaptability scores
- Time to proficiency in new roles or processes
- Retention rates during periods of organizational change

Conduct Regular Pulse Surveys

Gather feedback from new hires to gauge their ability to adapt and remain resilient:

- Assess comfort levels with change and uncertainty
- Measure perceived support for navigating challenges
- Identify areas where additional resources or training may be needed

Monitor Long-term Performance

Track the long-term impact of change and resilience-focused onboarding:

- Compare performance metrics of employees who underwent the new onboarding process versus previous methods
- Analyze career progression and internal mobility rates
- Assess employee engagement levels during times of organizational change

Resistance to New Approaches

Address potential resistance to change within the
HR team and broader organization:

- Communicate the benefits of incorporating change and
resilience into onboarding
- Provide training for HR professionals on new
onboarding methodologies
- Showcase early successes and positive outcomes to
build buy-in

Balancing Consistency and Flexibility

Strike a balance between maintaining consistent
onboarding experiences and allowing for flexibility:

- Establish core onboarding elements that remain
constant
- Create guidelines for customizing onboarding
experiences while adhering to key principles
- Regularly review and update onboarding processes to
ensure relevance and effectiveness

Resource Constraints

Navigate potential resource limitations when
implementing new onboarding approaches:

- Prioritize high-impact changes that can be implemented
with existing resources
- Explore partnerships with external providers for
specialized content or technology

- Leverage internal expertise by involving employees in the design and delivery of onboarding activities

Embracing change and fostering resilience in onboarding is essential for preparing new hires to thrive in today's dynamic business environment. By incorporating flexible structures, emphasizing adaptability, and teaching resilience skills, organizations can create onboarding experiences that set employees up for long-term success. As we continue to face unprecedented challenges and opportunities, the ability to navigate change and bounce back from setbacks will be crucial for both individual and organizational success.

By implementing the strategies outlined in this section, HR professionals can transform their onboarding processes to not only welcome new employees but also equip them with the mindset and skills necessary to excel in an ever-changing workplace. As organizations prioritize change management and resilience in their onboarding approaches, they will cultivate a workforce that is better prepared to adapt, innovate, and drive success in the face of future challenges.

Leading the Way: The Role of Onboarding Professionals

In the ever-evolving landscape of human resources and talent management, the role of Onboarding Professionals has emerged as a critical component in ensuring the success of new hires and the overall effectiveness of an organization's onboarding process. These seasoned professionals play a pivotal role in shaping the first impressions and experiences of new employees, setting the tone for their entire journey within the company. This section explores the multifaceted responsibilities, key competencies, and strategic importance of Onboarding Professionals in today's competitive business environment.

The Strategic Importance of Onboarding Professionals

Bridging the Gap Between Recruitment and Integration

Onboarding Professionals serve as the crucial link between the recruitment process and the full integration of new employees into the organization. They ensure a seamless transition from candidate to team member, minimizing the time it takes for new hires to become productive contributors.

Championing Organizational Culture

These professionals are the frontline ambassadors of the company's culture, values, and mission. They play a vital role in communicating and reinforcing these elements to new hires, ensuring that they align with the organization's ethos from day one.

Driving Employee Engagement and Retention

By creating positive first impressions and fostering a sense of belonging, Onboarding Professionals significantly impact employee engagement and long-term retention. Their efforts contribute to reduced turnover rates and increased employee satisfaction.

Key Responsibilities of Onboarding Professionals

Designing and Implementing Comprehensive Onboarding Programs

Onboarding Professionals are responsible for crafting holistic onboarding experiences that address all aspects of a new hire's integration, including:

- Orientation to company policies and procedures
- Introduction to team members and key stakeholders
- Training on essential tools and systems
- Familiarization with the company's products, services, and industry position

Customizing Onboarding Experiences

Recognizing that one size does not fit all, these professionals tailor onboarding programs to meet the specific needs of different roles, departments, and individual new hires. This personalized approach ensures that each employee receives the most relevant and impactful onboarding experience possible.

Coordinating Cross-Functional Collaboration

Onboarding Professionals act as the central point of contact, coordinating efforts across various departments such as HR, IT, Facilities, and individual business units. This collaboration ensures a cohesive and comprehensive onboarding process.

Mentoring and Supporting New Hires

Beyond the initial orientation, these officers provide ongoing support and guidance to new employees, serving as a trusted resource throughout their early tenure with the company.

Measuring and Analyzing Onboarding Effectiveness

Using data-driven approaches, Onboarding Professionals continuously assess the impact of their programs, gathering feedback and metrics to refine and improve the onboarding process.

Essential Competencies for Onboarding Professionals

Strong Communication and Interpersonal Skills

The ability to effectively communicate with individuals at all levels of the organization is crucial. Onboarding Professionals must be adept at both verbal and written communication, with a talent for making complex information accessible and engaging.

Cultural Intelligence and Empathy

In today's diverse workplaces, these professionals must possess a high degree of cultural intelligence and empathy, ensuring that onboarding programs are inclusive and respectful of various backgrounds and perspectives.

Project Management Expertise

Coordinating multiple onboarding initiatives simultaneously requires excellent project management skills, including the ability to prioritize tasks, manage timelines, and allocate resources effectively.

Technological Proficiency

As onboarding processes increasingly leverage digital tools and platforms, Onboarding Professionals must be comfortable with a range of technologies, from learning management systems to virtual reality onboarding experiences.

Data Analysis and Interpretation

The ability to collect, analyze, and interpret data related to onboarding effectiveness is essential for continuous improvement and demonstrating the value of onboarding initiatives to stakeholders.

Challenges Faced by Onboarding Professionals

Balancing Standardization and Personalization

One of the primary challenges is striking the right balance between maintaining consistent onboarding standards across the organization while also providing personalized experiences for individual new hires.

Adapting to Remote and Hybrid Work Environments

The shift towards remote and hybrid work models has necessitated a reimagining of traditional onboarding practices. Onboarding Professionals must innovate to create engaging virtual onboarding experiences that foster connection and belonging in distributed teams.

Keeping Pace with Organizational Changes

In rapidly evolving businesses, these professionals must constantly update their onboarding programs to reflect changes in company structure, processes, and technologies.

Managing Stakeholder Expectations

Onboarding Professionals often need to navigate competing priorities and expectations from various stakeholders, including new hires, hiring managers, and senior leadership.

Best Practices for Onboarding Professionals

Embrace a Growth Mindset

Continuously seek out new knowledge, trends, and best practices in onboarding and talent management to stay at the forefront of the field.

Foster Strong Partnerships

Build and maintain strong relationships with key stakeholders across the organization to ensure smooth collaboration and support for onboarding initiatives.

Leverage Technology Wisely

Utilize technology to enhance and streamline the onboarding process, but always balance it with human touch and personal interactions.

Regularly solicit feedback from new hires, managers, and other stakeholders to identify areas for improvement and refine onboarding programs accordingly.

Champion Diversity, Equity, and Inclusion

Ensure that onboarding programs are inclusive and welcoming to individuals from all backgrounds, promoting a diverse and equitable workplace culture.

The Future of Onboarding Professionals

As organizations continue to recognize the critical importance of effective onboarding in driving employee engagement and retention, the role of Onboarding Professionals is likely to evolve and expand. We can expect to see:

- Increased focus on long-term employee success beyond the initial onboarding period
- Greater integration of artificial intelligence and machine learning in personalizing onboarding experiences
- Enhanced emphasis on measuring and demonstrating the ROI of onboarding initiatives
- Expanded responsibilities in areas such as employer branding and talent retention strategies

Onboarding Professionals play a pivotal role in shaping the future success of organizations by ensuring that new hires are effectively integrated, engaged, and set up for long-term success. By mastering the complexities of modern onboarding, embracing innovation, and continuously refining their approaches, these professionals lead the way in creating positive, impactful first impressions that resonate throughout an employee's tenure. As the business landscape continues to evolve, the strategic importance of Onboarding Professionals in driving organizational success will only continue to grow.